Best wishes
John Ed Pearce

This Place
Called
Kentucky

THIS PLACE CALLED
KENTUCKY

PHOTOGRAPHY BY DAN DRY

ESSAYS BY JOHN ED PEARCE

THE SULGRAVE PRESS
in association with
BUTLER BOOKS

Executive Editors: John S. Moremen and William S. Butler
Captions and Art Direction: John S. Moremen
Consulting Editor: James S. Pope, Jr.
Editor: Amy Spears
Production: Butler Books
Production Assistant: Justin Estes

Second Printing, 1995

ISBN 0-9624086-6-2

Printed in Canada

Laura Lee Brown

Without her vision and interest, this definitive photography book on the Commonwealth of Kentucky could never have been published. A native of Louisville and member of the distinguished Brown family of Brown Forman Corporation, she is a mother, an artist, a photographer, and a world traveler.

The Sulgrave Press gratefully acknowledges her active participation in the concept and development of *This Place Called Kentucky*.

THIS PLACE CALLED KENTUCKY

Kentucky is a land so varied in appearance, in mood and in background that it fits almost any preconception one may have of it. It is the home of dust-blackened coal miners, sunburned tobacco farmers, seven-foot basketballers, and flat-eyed hill dwellers. It is also the home of historic mansions and auctioneers who sell, in elegant surroundings, million-dollar colts to eastern bankers and foreign potentates.

It is a land of contradictions and inconsistencies. It is the Bluegrass State, though only the central region around Lexington is called the Bluegrass, and even there, little bluegrass is grown any more, having given way to hardier strains. It isn't really blue, anyhow.

Kentuckians proclaim great pride in their state, and vow great loyalty to it. The motto on the state seal declares: United We Stand, Divided We Fall, but the state is and has often been sharply divided. Indeed, Kentucky is a collection of radi-

cally different regions which regard each other with tolerance and sometimes suspicion, held together by legend, history and accident of geography.

No state was more painfully divided by the Civil War than Kentucky. Other states debated the issue of slavery and turned their faces to the North or South. Kentucky fought over the issue for half a century and went both ways, tearing itself in two. It sent more than twice as many men to the Union armies as to the Confederacy, but much of it remained southern at heart. It is significant that both Abraham Lincoln, President of the United States, and Jefferson Davis, President of the Confederacy, were born in Kentucky. Throughout the war, Kentucky was in the Union, though a governor resigned rather than remain neutral and there was for a time a Confederate state capitol. But, following the war, thanks in part to harsh policies on the part of federal officers, the state exploded with sympathy for the South, leading one historian to lament that it was the only government in history to join the loser after the loss.

Kentuckians are remarkable for their devotion to the counties in which they live, and are often identified by the region from which they come. Eastern Kentucky considers itself a section apart, as do other sections. Louisville, the largest city, is often resented by people "out in the state", and in turn considers itself superior. Frankfort is the capital of Kentucky, and Louisville its economic center, but Lexington is probably its heart. This is partly because it is the home of the University of Kentucky, home of the Big Blue, the basketball team that for half a century has symbolized Kentucky's hopes and pride. And Kentuckians like to think of Lexington and its surrounding necklace of horse farms, white fences, frolicking thoroughbreds and Keeneland Race Course, all elements of that picturesque Bluegrass mystique, as typical of Kentucky. It isn't, but that is not the point.

Then there is Western Kentucky, which may include all of the land west of Bowling Green and Owensboro, depending on how you define it. What many people call Western Kentucky contains much of the Pennyroyal, or Pennyrile, section which stretches from the land around Lake Cumberland on the east to Logan County on the west, and then northward to the Ohio River, and includes a large coalfield, and the hilly region around Mammoth Cave in Edmonson County.

But when people refer to Western Kentucky they often mean the entire western part of the state. It is principally farm land, stretching to the banks of the Mississippi and at one time containing cotton plantations. The region includes the far western counties purchased from the Indians by Andrew Jackson and called, in a burst of imagination, the Jackson Purchase, long known as the Gibraltar of Democracy (meaning, of course, the Democratic Party.) During the trouble caused by the North (sometimes referred to as the Civil War,) much of Western Kentucky sided with the Confederacy.

Along the southern part of the state is a series of large, man-made lakes which attract a welcome flow of tourists, as does the state parks system, purportedly one of the finest in the nation. Northern Kentucky, like Eastern Kentucky, feels that it is neglected by the rest of the state, and is somewhat oriented toward Cincinnati. The region is regarded by the rest of the state as suspiciously northern.

The state pays little attention to its history of violence, feuds and duels. These left a raw residue in such labels as Bloody Harlan and Bloody Breathitt counties, but the state today enjoys a relatively minor homicide rate.

Kentucky is the home of Bourbon whiskey; you can produce Bourbon in other states, but Kentucky Bourbon is the product and, by law, you cannot produce it out of the state and use "Kentucky" on the label. Kentucky has long been known, too, for its white lightning, or moonshine whiskey, and during the prohibition era Golden Pond, a hamlet in Western Kentucky, was famous from New Orleans to Chicago and Detroit for its mellow moonshine.

Kentucky was also the home of the famed Henry Clay, who tried to evade the slavery controversy through an economic compromise, and probably lost the presidency in the process; and his fiery cousin Cassius, an unlikely abolitionist in pre-Civil War central Kentucky. The state is known for its rugged frontiersmen: Daniel Boone, Jim Harrod, Simon Kenton, and George Rogers Clark. But it has also sent to Washington eight justices of the Supreme Court, including the redoubtable John Marshall Harlan, Louis Brandeis, Stanley Reed and Fred Vinson. Probably the most popular African-American of the 20th century, boxing champion Muhammed Ali (born Cassius Clay) is a Kentuckian.

Kentucky is the home, as one might suspect, of the famed Kentucky Colonel, immortalized, curiously enough, by Harland Sanders, the developer of Kentucky Fried Chicken, who was born, unfortunately, in Indiana. The title has little significance, and anyone who knows a governor can be one.

Kentucky is basketball mad. When the Big

Blue is playing in Lexington's Rupp Arena, named for revered UK coach Adolf Rupp, true Kentuckians will attend if they can fight their way in, and crowds fill Freedom Hall when the University of Louisville Cardinals take the floor. Each spring the best high-school basketball teams from the state's sixteen regions meet in what is affectionately known as the Sweet Sixteen. Men remember playing in the Sweet Sixteen as others remember war experiences or women of their youth.

Kentuckians are religious, often aggressively so, yet the state's economy has historically depended on man's frailties — whiskey, tobacco and horse racing, with coal thrown in for good measure. Natives who have been driven by fate to live elsewhere for a while give Derby parties in their nostalgia and invite in outlanders to enjoy country ham, beaten biscuits and Mint Juleps, a powerful drink they seldom touch at other times. And they stand, facing the television set, and weep when the band plays "My Old Kentucky Home," to which relatively few know all the words save for the rousing chorus.

For whatever reasons, Kentuckians, who are as varied and as intriguing as the land from which they spring, love their state, and outsiders can put themselves in harm's way by speaking poorly of it. As the late Governor Happy Chandler said, "Wherever I have traveled in this land, I never met a Kentuckian who wasn't going home."

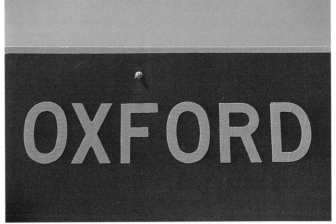

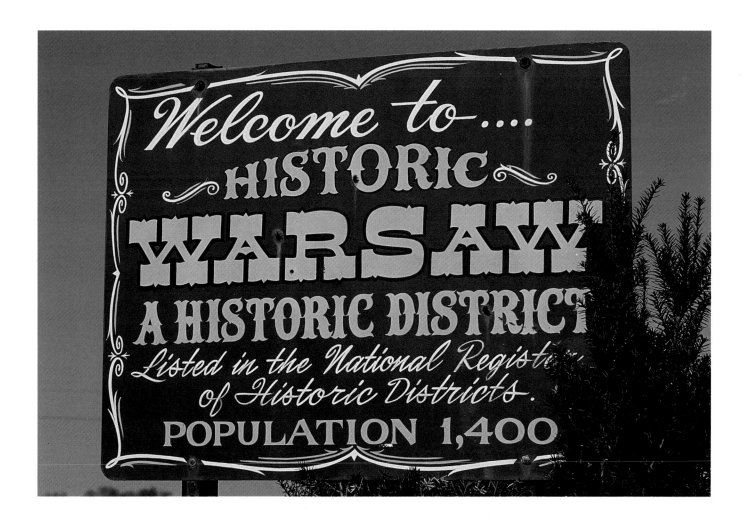

It is not necessary to travel abroad to see the great cities of Europe, because most of them are in Kentucky. The Commonwealth was settled primarily by the English and Scots-Irish, with a large influx of Germans in the mid-1800s.

One of the last covered bridges in Kentucky is the Goddard Bridge in Fleming County.

Kentucky is known worldwide as the home of the thoroughbred.

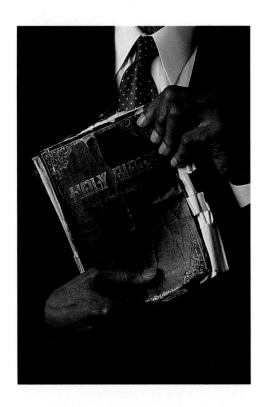

(Both pages) Kentucky hands at work and play.

Fort Knox, just southwest of Louisville, is the U.S. Army's Armor Center, and the site of America's gold depository.

My Old Kentucky Home, Bardstown, Kentucky.

Kentucky crafts include folk art originals, such as these decorative walking sticks at the Folk Art Museum in Morehead, Kentucky.

The State Capitol in Frankfort, built in 1824 by Gideon Shryock, after fire destroyed the original capitol building.

The twin spires of Churchill Downs, the home of the Kentucky Derby.

LOUISVILLE AND JEFFERSON COUNTY

People who live in Louisville seem quite pleased with it. A poll in 1994 found that even teenagers thought it was a nice place to live. They even liked their schools. People who have lived in Louisville for a while often resign their jobs rather than be transferred, and many factory officials moving here from the North seem to think they have died and gone to heaven.

Residents give widely assorted reasons for this affection. It just seems an easy place to live. It's cooler than cities to the south and warmer than those to the north. It's a short flight from New York, Washington, Chicago, Atlanta and Florida. Taxes are reasonable, housing is relatively inexpensive, traffic is light and the schools are good. Besides the University of Louisville, the community boasts five colleges and two of the South's major seminaries, Baptist and Presbyterian. The Louisville Free Public Library has been hailed as one of the most innovative in the country. Louisville is also a strong neighborhood town. Neighborhood associations lobby City Hall, form Block Watches, hold fairs and sponsor beautification projects.

For people who like the outdoors, there is the Ohio River (more than 10,000 boats are licensed in the area), a noted system of parks designed by famed architect Frederick Law Olmsted, and golf courses dotting the city and its surrounding Jefferson County. And, of course, there is horse racing at Churchill Downs, home of the legendary Kentucky Derby. And basketball is everywhere.

Like most cities, Louisville is a town in transition. At the end of World War II it was a midsize industrial city, dominated by a handful of large industries and a dozen or so old families. But many of the old families have died out, sold out, fallen apart or moved away. The Bingham family sold its long-dominant Courier-Journal to Gannett, Inc., and the Bingham and Norton radio and television stations were sold to outside chains. An aggressive group of young entrepeneurs, including David Jones, Wendell Cherry, John Y. Brown, Jr. and

David Grissom, shouldered their way onto the scene with such firms as Humana and KFC. New tall buildings changed the skyline and the town's economy shifted from heavy to service industry.

Two other developments changed the tenor of life as much as the shift in industry. School integration was accomplished, but not without considerable unrest and some white migration to the eastern suburbs and surrounding counties of Louisville. At the same time, the town's vibrant shopping district, centered around Fourth and Walnut streets, began to lose retail business to suburban malls. The growth outward from the center was spurred by construction of belt and interstate highways. Dozens of small incorporated cities sprang up, hampering efforts to merge Louisville and Jefferson County.

The arts flourish in spite of the financial problems common to the arts in most cities. The Kentucky Center for the Arts would be a crown jewel for any city, and brings people from across the state to touring Broadway plays and performances of the Louisville Orchestra, Ballet and the Kentucky Opera. Nearby Actors Theatre has gained national recognition, including a special Tony award for its Humana-sponsored festival of original plays, many later produced on Broadway. The J.B. Speed Art Museum is noted for the breadth of its collection and the frequent special exhibits.

Despite school integration and the generally calm acceptance of laws opening public accomodations in the 1960's, Louisville is divided along lines not written but understood. Western Louisville ("The West End") contains most of the town's African-Americans, the East End and the eastern suburbs control much of the community wealth, while the southern and southwestern areas are relatively blue collar. As one writer put it, "The East End has the money, the South End has the muscle, the West End has the problems." Neither sympathetic city government nor the supportive attitude of the influential Courier-Journal have been able to correct this to any appreciable degree.

Those who sniff that Louisville is more a beer-and-baseball than a Bach-and-Beethoven town might be right, although it might be closer to the mark to call it a beer-and-basketball haven. The town is rabid in its support of the University of Louisville basketball squads led by Hall-of-Fame coach Denny Crum, and fans tear the place apart when the twice national champion Cardinals defeat the five-time national champion Wildcats from the University of Kentucky. The Redbirds, the minor-league farm club of the St. Louis Cardinals, draw fair-sized crowds as well.

People seem to have a hard time classifying Louisville. Southerners view it as northern or midwestern, and people from the East think of it as a southern place of mint juleps and magnolia, partly because many only see it at Derby time, when the city tends to put its southern foot forward. In a sense, the Derby is for visitors, while many locals enjoy more the Derby Festival, which takes place in the two weeks before the Big Race, and features such hoopla as a parade, a steamboat race between paddle-wheelers, a balloon race, a short version of the marathon, fireworks and endless food fairs, dances and parties. Many locals prefer the Kentucky Oaks, a race for fillies on the day before the Derby, to the big race itself, partly because good seats are easier to find and the crowd is smaller.

From its beginnings, location has to a large extent defined Louisville. The original settlement was founded by George Rogers Clark, when he came down the Ohio in 1777 on his way to attack the British at Vincennes, Caskaskia and Cahokia, in the brilliant campaign which won the northwest territory for the embattled colonies. Returning from his historic victory, Clark helped to found the village that became Louisville, spending much of his remaining life at Locust Grove, his sister's home where he died, one of the greatest, and most unappreciated, heroes of his country's birth.

Just as the river caused Louisville to exist, so did it cause it to flourish. Flatboats and keelboats carrying early settlers and produce could shoot the Falls of the Ohio, a series of rapids created by Devonian rock formations, on their trip downriver, but could not get back upstream against its rocks

In 1779 Louisville was named for Louis XVI of France as a token of gratitude for French help to the colonies during the Revolutionary War. The French, however, did not think as highly of him; he was beheaded in the 1790s.

and currents. Their cargoes had to be hauled around the Falls for the upriver trip, before a canal was built to let traffic pass both ways. Storehouses, warehouses, and boat building and supply facilities soon sprang up along the shore and a town took shape.

Still, Lexington, situated at the crossroads of the state's roads and turnpikes, was Kentucky's center of commerce and largest town until the coming of the steamboat, when commerce shifted from roads to rivers. The Ohio River became an artery of regional and even international trade, and Louisville mushroomed. But while its location had earned it the early name of The Ponds Settlement, its location on the banks of the Ohio also assured its growth as a commercial center.

In the years before the Civil War, railroads began shouldering aside river traffic, but the founding of the Louisville & Nashville Railroad made Louisville even more prominent in north-south trade. Founded by James Guthrie and built by Milton Smith, the L&N gave Louisville a decided edge in the fight for commerce. And it was commerce, more than patriotism, that underlay

Louisville's loyalty to the Union in the Civil War. It was a concern for commerce that prompted editor Henry Watterson to urge conciliation with the North and the industrialization of the South. While much of Kentucky, torn apart by the war and its violent aftermath, sank into economic lethargy, Louisville flourished as a pivotal point of North-South transportation. The L&N gave it a distinct advantage in the competition for trade.

Louisville's economy has been something of a roller-coaster. Steady growth in the years following the Civil War was followed by slower activity in the first years of the 20th century. The town fell under the influence of a stodgy Board of Trade and financiers such as the eccentric James Brown, whose BancoKentucky rode the mild boom of the early Twenties, only to fall victim to the Depression and Brown's unusual practices, including his purchase of the meteoric *Herald-Post*, which flared, flourished and then fell in battle with the more solid *Courier-Journal*.

Louisville rode out the Depression in fairly good fashion and hummed into the boom that came with World War II. New plants of such firms as Ford and General Electric sparked a postwar boom, but with the 1960s, the boom slowed as more and more people and retail stores headed for the suburbs.

Ford, GE, tobacco and distilleries are still major factors in the economy of the overall community. But the core city has become increasingly the site of service industries. Columbia/HCA, Humana, the downtown hospital-medical complex, hotels, office buildings, the headquarters of the Presbyterian Church USA and development of the arts complex along Main Street have, to an extent, revived downtown and made Louisville more white than blue collar.

Louisville's status as Kentucky's largest and most preeminent city, as well as its prosperity, have somewhat set it apart from the rest of the state. Since the Civil War, Kentucky has been relatively poor, and its government must stretch a little revenue to cover a host of needs. The rest of the state tends to resent money spent on relatively rich Louisville, and Louisville taxpayers complain that they bear an unfair portion of the state tax burden. And while much of the rural economy of the state remains stagnant, the Golden Triangle bounded by Louisville, Lexington and Covington enjoys most of the state's economic growth.

The Farnsley-Moremen House, in southwest Jefferson County, was built on the banks of the Ohio River in 1793 and was in the Moremen family for over 150 years. It has recently been restored by Jefferson County. During the Civil War, scion Alanson Moremen had one nephew in the Union and one in the Confederate Army, but when they came to Riverview (the house name), he would not allow them to wear their uniforms inside, considering his home a place of peace.

You can always tell a winner. Jockey Jerry Bailey gives the horse racing equivalent of a high five to the crowd, crossing the finish line at Churchill Downs in the proper place— first.

Owsley Brown II, President of Brown Forman Corporation, is the fourth generation of his family to run the multi-million dollar business, which started as a Bourbon distillery in 1870. He stands before Actors Theatre of Kentucky, one of the crown jewels of American theater, which he has helped flourish for decades.

From its mooring at the foot of Third Street in Louisville, the old paddlewheeler, Belle of Louisville, *plies the waterways of the Ohio River. The boat was purchased in the 1950s by the Jefferson County Judge-Executive for $30,000, and then many thousands more were spent on its restoration, much to the disgust of some vocal taxpayers. They love it now, however, and it is jammed with crowds in the summertime. During Derby Week, the* Belle *and the* Delta Queen *race up and down the Ohio, each using sometimes questionable, but always good-natured, tactics to win the race.*

An outstanding example of modern architecture is the Kentucky Center for the Arts, where performances of the well-known Louisville Orchestra, Kentucky Opera and Louisville Ballet take place along with many touring Broadway shows. The late civic leader, Wendell Cherry, was one of the driving forces in building and furnishing the center with art and sculpture.

Lynn Cralle, one of the owners of a very avant garde art gallery in Louisville, has started many an unknown artist on the path to commercial success. Here she poses with Rodney Hatfield, an artist and member of a successful blues band. Rodney's family was part of the famous Hatfield and McCoy feuds of Eastern Kentucky.

A group of young racing fans celebrate Derby Day at Churchill Downs, where the Kentucky Derby has been run continuously since 1875.

The annual St. James Art Festival, where artists come from far and wide to display their crafts, is held in a beautiful section of the city known as Old Louisville.

In western Louisville, the Dirt Bowl brings high school, college and pro basketballers to showcase their talents before large crowds. The playground is in constant use.

A gigantic Ferris wheel rises above the State Fair and Kentucky Kingdom, Louisville's fast-growing amusement park.

Each year, the Zachary Taylor cemetery in Jefferson County is the site of Memorial Day ceremonies for the war dead. Here, a young girl carries the flag.

Behind the spring dogwoods of Kentucky is the house where Jefferson Davis married the daughter of President Zachary Taylor. On her honeymoon in Louisiana three months later, she caught malaria and died.

Mary Bingham, widow of Louisville Courier-Journal *publisher Barry Bingham, Sr., has been one of the foremost philanthropists in Kentucky, giving generously to many varied causes.*

The Derby Museum Ball.

Belgravia Court, Old Louisville.

The steeplechase races at the Hardscuffle Farm in Oldham County have been the occasion of fund raising for the Kentucky Opera for the last 20 years. Tailgating and picnics prevail in a happy, social atmosphere.

Two gentlemen of the hunt discuss the day over a julep. Fox hunting is an activity enjoyed by several Hunts in the state, although the hunters rarely catch and seldom see the fox, nullifying the blood sport feature of the activity. The social aspects remain undiminished.

Barney Bright, Louisville sculptor and artist, is nationally known and respected. His outdoor sculpture stands in many public places. Below, hot air balloons over Louisville.

The old Louisville Water Works is a landmark on the banks of the Ohio River. Built between 1856 and 1860, the Works features a distinctive tower, the crown of which is adorned with 13 carved statues.

Pat Day, one of America's best jockeys, tells it all with his first Derby victory in 1993. As can be seen from the tote board in the background, he wasn't on the favorite. His horse, Lil E Tee, paid $35.60.

A groom washes down one of his charges on the backside.

Victory celebration.

Wagner's Pharmacy near Churchill Downs is a hangout for track people at all hours of the day and night. They serve the original power breakfast.

There are lots of box seats, but they're hard to come by.

At the annual Derby Festival steamboat race, Jim Stites, a prominent retired attorney, and Cy Mackinnon, the former president of the Louisville Courier-Journal, *discuss the day's events.*

General John B. Castleman, who fought as a Confederate general in the Civil War, rides his famous "green horse" in the Cherokee Triangle area of Louisville. The statue loses its green color when cleaned, and is frequently decorated with holiday wreaths.

Peter Morrin, the Director of the Speed Museum in Louisville, and Portrait of a Woman *by Rembrandt, pose in the museum. Under Mr. Morrin's leadership, there has been renewed vitality at the Speed where a number of new galleries and exhibits have been created in recent years.*

The folk artist, Marvin Finn, has found his niche in animal art, and here he peers through one of his famous painted birds.

A horse-drawn carriage awaits late-night passengers in front of the former Levy Brothers building, which now houses the Old Spaghetti Factory.

The educational system of the state utilizes computers to the same degree that McGuffey's Reader was once used by prior generations.

The Humana Corporation was started as a nursing home venture by two Louisville lawyers, David Jones and Wendell Cherry, in the late 1960s. Over the years it evolved into one of the largest hospital companies in the country and is now a giant health insurance organization. David Jones, the chairman and a Louisville native, stands before the unusual building designed by Michael Graves. Jones' industrious participation in the development of the downtown and riverfront area of the city has been determined and successful.

Michael Graves designed the Humana Building, an enormous structure of marble and steel which creates visual interest in Louisville's downtown architecture.

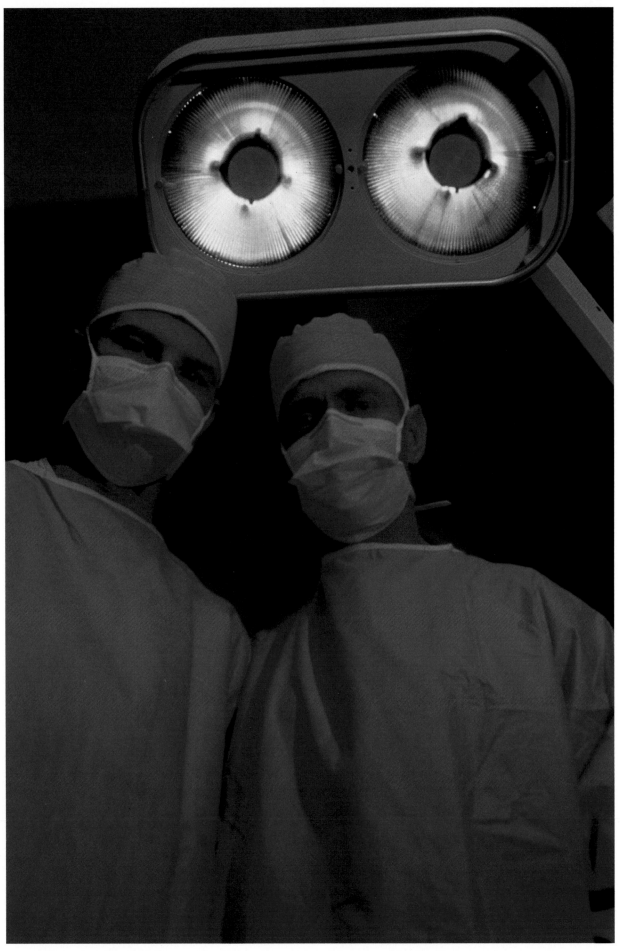

Louisville is an internationally recognized center for surgery on hearts and hands. Here, two surgeons assess a potential patient.

The biggest rivalry in Kentucky sports is the annual pitting of the University of Louisville and the University of Kentucky's basketball teams against each other. Because of their competition in recruiting, the two teams rarely played in years past except in NCAA tournaments. It took pressure from the legislature of Kentucky to ensure an annual contest.

JEFFERSON COUNTY KOREAN WAR CASUALTIES

NALD LEE ABNEY • RAY M. ADAMS • JOHN J. ASPDEN • WILMER BAILEY
LIAM E. BARNES • NORMAN F. BARR • COURTENAY BARRETT • JOHN H. BASHAM
FFORD D. BEASLEY • WILLIE BECKLEY • JAMES E. BEVILLE • JAMES H. BLAIR
FFORD R. BOGARD • ALFRED G. BORKLAND JR • RAYMOND TRAMMELL BOWERS
ARLES W. BRAGG • CHARLES W. BROWN • MEADE M. BROWN • PAUL C. BRYANT
D E. BURKS • JACK W. CAMPBELL • JACKIE A. CAMPBELL • GRANT D. CARTER JR.
RMAN G. CAWTHORN • WILLIAM R. CLUFF • CHARLES COLEMAN • JOHN SOULARD CO
RGE W. CONNER • HAROLD R. COOPER • ELLIS H. COPELAND • DAVID E. CRABTR
ESTER DAVIDO   • WILLIAM H. DEAN • EUGENE DEDMAN • HAROLD A. DUNCAN
DE G. DUNN •   N. EBERLE • JUNIOR E. ELLEFSON • JAMES A. ELLIOTT
WARD RICHARD EVANS   AYMOND FAIRCHILD • JAMES CARL FARRIS • HERMAN G. FELHOE
ARK FELTNER • CHESTER A. FIELDS • KENNETH R. FLOWERS • PATRICK H. FORD JR.
OMAS O. FOWLER • HARVEY L. FREY • JOHN WILLIAM GAHAN • GEORGE M. GALES
NRY C. GAMBLE • KOELING B. GARDNER • MURREL GARVIN • RICHARD E. GERRISH JR
ARLES EVERETT GETTINGS • JAMES GIDRON • GEORGE D. GILLESPIE JR • VERNON E. GIRDLE
ARLES C. GOFF • MELVIN EUGENE GOLDSMITH • ROBERT V. GOLDSMITH
SEPH M. GREENWELL JR • JAMES ALLEN GREGORY • GEORGE H. GROOMES
UGLAS H. HAAG • GARLAND R. HALL • LEONARD J. HARMON • JACK RAY HARRIS
VID THAMES HEER • JOHN F. HERDLICK • ALLAN BENNETT HOAGLARD • WILLIAM G. HOLLO
LLIAM T. JACKSON • CHARLES EDWARD JARRETT • CHARLES W. JOHNSON
CHARD W. JOHNSON • VINCENT J. JOHNSON • THOMAS JOYCE JR • CHARLES R. KAST
NALD J. KEEFE • CHARLES E. KEELEY • MERLIN R. KEHRER • LAWRENCE BERTRAND KEL
ANK C. KENNEDY • WILLIAM O. KOLB • LOUIS CASPER KRAUS • DANIEL L. KREMER
RL B. KRESEN • CLYDE E. LAMKINS • VERNON S. LEDFORD • ALBERT LEFTWICH
LPH L. LEITNER • WILLIAM R. LINER • STEWART W. LONG • FRED E. MACK JR.
HN J MAGDA • ROBERT R. MARTIN • JOSEPH J. MATTIMORE • GERALD J. MATTINGL

The Korean War Memorial in Jefferson County was not constructed until 1993, nearly 40 years after the fighting was over. Someone has left a small bow on the name of a Jefferson County man who died in that almost forgotten war.

Two zebras gaze from their exhibit at the Lousville Zoo which was founded in 1969 with a grant from J. Graham Brown, owner of the Brown Hotel. There are 16,000 animals on the premises.

Tobacco leaves are examined by a tobacco company inspector. The tobacco industry employs about 5,000 people in the state, not counting the thousands of farmers who grow the product.

Croquet at Hardscuffle

Derby Day also marks the start of Hat Season in Louisville.

NORTHERN KENTUCKY

People from Eastern and Western Kentucky complain that their regions are overlooked and neglected, but if anybody has a right to complain it's the Northern Kentuckians. Not everyone knows it, but the land west of Ashland, north of Paris and east of Bedford contains some of the most interesting country in the state.

Stretching along the Ohio River for half the length of this long state, the region may be divided into three general areas; the riverfront, the suburban areas behind it, and the museum pieces, old towns which look as though they had been plucked out of yesterday and set down in today.

Take Maysville, for instance. Good town. To get a decent drink you have to go across the river into Ohio territory, but otherwise, it is an intriguing town, with remarkable architecture, historic buildings and passenger train service. Not every small town has a passenger train these days. But to get to Lexington you have to take US 68 as it winds through Washington, Kentucky, which, incidentally,

is another interesting stop. It is made up chiefly of log houses which look pretty much as they did when Simon Kenton sold the land to two Virginians who formed a town and named it for George Washington. It was for years the county seat, but today is only a surburb of Maysville. It is a big tourist attraction, though.

Simon Kenton was a character. He got into a fight over a girl, thought he had killed his rival, ran away from his Virginia home and headed west. By the time he found out that he had only knocked the rival unconscious and was not wanted by the law, he had become a dyed-in-the-wool frontiersman. He is said to have saved Daniel Boone's life twice in one day while they were fighting Indians, and is reported to have told the famous woodsman, "Damn, Boone, I'm getting tired of carrying you."

Not far upstream from Maysville is Vanceburg, which is noteworthy, if for no other reason, for having the only statue to Union soldiers in Kentucky. As you might surmise, Lewis County was a Union hotbed during the Civil War, 107 men died in their ranks, and the town and county have been Republican ever since. People here used to fish mussels out of the Ohio River and make buttons from them, but plastic ran them out of business.

Jesse Stuart gave the region around Carter and Greenup Counties, south and east of Maysville's Mason County, some brief fame with his novels and poetry. Jesse wrote movingly about the plain people who lived back in the hills where the roads were rough and the living was basic. His stories about foxes and corn cribs and bull-tongued plows brought quite a bit of attention to the area.

Quite a bit has happened over the years down the road in Morehead, in Rowan County, though. It was in Morehead that the bloody Martin-Tolliver feud almost ruined the town until a man named Logan got some men together and killed most of the Tolliver side, which cooled the fighting. But that isn't all that Morehead is known for. In time the little teachers' school became Morehead State University, and Cave Run Lake, down at the south border of the county, has become a major tourist and sportsman's attraction.

Augusta, just downriver from Maysville (you can drive it in 20-30 minutes) is another of these old river towns that looks as if it had been lifted out of history. The place just has a romantic, old fashioned look about it; twice recently, film companies have used Augusta as the site of movies about Mark Twain's Hannibal, Missouri, since it is said to look more like the popular idea of Mark Twain's day than the real Hannibal does today. There is a whole row of beautiful old homes along the bluff above the river, and it is also a port for one of the few ferries remaining in operation between Kentucky and Ohio. Gertrude Schweier used to run a boarding house for riverboat men there on Main Street, the last one on the river.

What is usually called Northern Kentucky is centered around the Covington area: Newport, Florence, Erlanger, Fort Thomas, and Fort Mitchell. Covington is Kentucky's third-largest city, but a lot of people think of it more as a suburb of Cincinnati. And it is, in a way, though it has a flavor all its own, with old breweries, most of them shut down now, a Riverside Drive lined with eye-popping, restored old homes built by river captains and merchants in the old river-shipping days, and a world-famous cathedral. People drive from all over to see its stained glass windows.

Newport, the upstream neighbor, is another story. Many big river towns, such as Cincinnati, used to have a "town across the river" where visiting salesmen or conventioneers could do some after-hours drinking, enjoy a little illegal gambling, and see a few girlie shows. Newport just had the bad (or good) luck to be situated across the river from Cincinnati, and after World War II, flowered as a sin city. It probably wasn't as wild as reputed, but mobsters from the north were said to be investing in establishments featuring illicit entertainment, and the townspeople became vexed. They complained to the governor, who then sent in state troopers. Soon indictments were flying around and people with such names as Tito and April Flowers were being interviewed by the press. Mlle. Flowers was said to take off her clothes, at least her outer garments, for the delectation of male onlookers. Mlle. Flowers, between clothes changes, was found in flagrante (well, not terribly flagrante) delicto with an ex-footballer who was running for sheriff and who later said he had no idea how he got there. It was that sort of time. The townspeople fumed, but the media had a ball.

The governor's purity crusade swept through Newport, sweeping out most of the sin and reducing the late-night tourism from across the river. The townsfolk became accustomed to the new, improved Newport and in time elected as mayor a bouncy, talkative fellow who spouted information and ideas with machine-gun speed and almost as much volume, a former television sales and repairman named, appropriately enough, Johnny TV Peluso.

Johnny set out to make Newport world class and world famous. He fell a little short. Critics charged that his bookkeeping was as unusual as some of his ideas, and before he could complete plans for a world-class restaurant suspended between Cincinnati and Newport, he was removed from office by the law. Newporters and reporters hated to see him leave, especially under such a cloud of controversy. His like has not been seen since. With sin, Mlle. Flowers, Tito and Johnny TV gone, Newport settled into a rather unexceptional calm, and old-timers sit and wonder where the big spenders go at night, and what happened to all those ladies who once shed apparel in public.

Downstream is Rabbit Hash which is a place, not a dish. It was once bigger than it is now, but the river washed a lot of it away. Probably the biggest thing there today is the general store, which does some business with people who stop by to ask how the place got its name. There are several versions, most of them having to do with a big flood that drove the rabbbits out of the bushes along the river and up into the fields where they were dispatched and eaten, first as fried rabbit, then as rabbit stew, then as — well, you know.

The fastest growing area of Northern Kentucky is the semi-suburban region south of Covington. Florence, for example, has for the past decade been one of the fastest-growning towns in Kentucky, much of the growth stemming from expansion of the big airport nearby named, to the annoyance of some locals, the Greater Cincinnati Airport. The local residents feel the airport should be named Northern Kentucky Regional Airport. That seems only right.

The stained glass window in the Cathedral Basilica of the Assumption in Covington is modeled after Notre Dame in Paris.

The tiny village of Washington had the grandiose idea of being the capital of the United States in 1800 when its population was 400 (and Louisville's was 200). Unfortunately, its population has declined since.

The steelmills around Newport are vital to the state's economy.

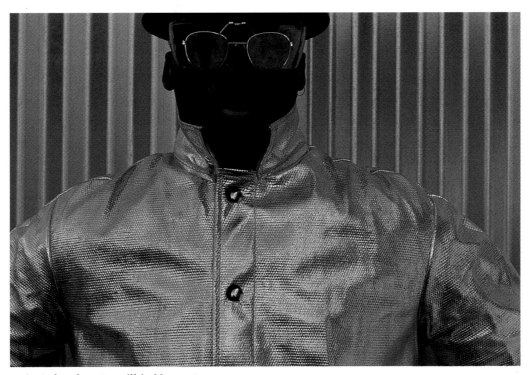

A steelworker at a mill in Newport.

Not far from the busy commercial area of Covington and Newport, nestled in a valley on the Ohio River, is the Rabbit Hash General Store, built in 1831, where everything from fishing tackle to doodads can be purchased. Because of its unusual name, the store appears in many books and articles about Kentucky. This one is no exception.

The riverboat ferry at Augusta is among the last ones on the Ohio River.

A tobacco farmer in Carroll County.

A house painter works to finish the job on this Covington home.

The Mayor of Millersburg and his chief aides sometimes meet on the lawn in the square. The Mayor, on the right, advises that they have answers for all questions.

The German influence in Covington is evident from the menu in this restaurant. During the Know-Nothing riots of the 1850s in Louisville, many German families migrated to Cincinnati, but some of them stayed on the south side of the Ohio River.

These spires grace Maysville, Kentucky. It was a thriving river town for many years and the center of commerce and steamboat traffic. The well-known singer Rosemary Clooney is from here.

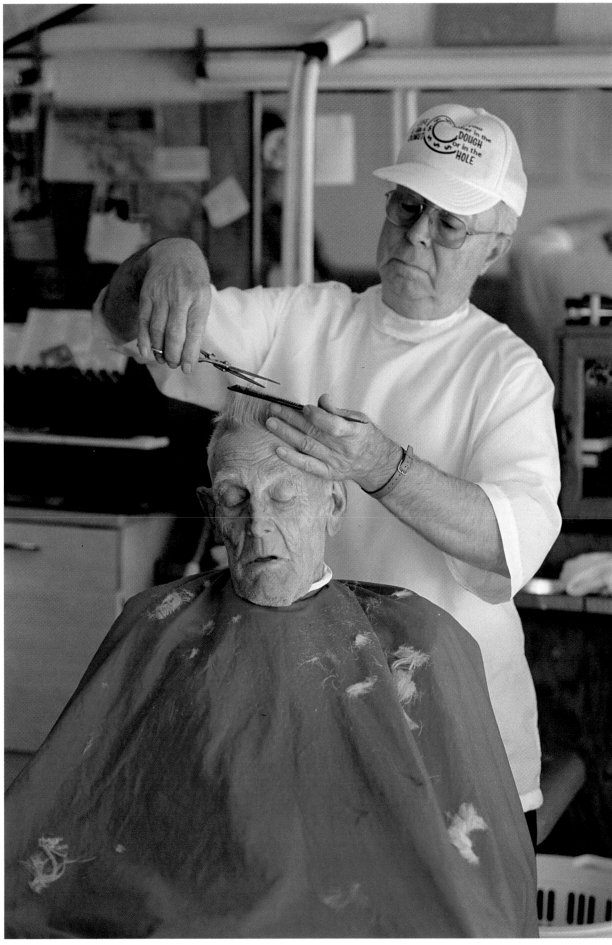

An elderly gentleman in Millersburg, Kentucky, enjoys his monthly haircut from a very correct barber.

Covington and Newport, across the river from Cincinnati, were centers of the brewing industry for many years. Although most of these enterprises went out of business from competition with the major beer companies, there are a few left. Oldenburg in Newport is one of them.

The Carroll Chimes Bell Tower in Covington has a 43-bell carillon and animated figures depicting the story of the Pied Piper of Hamelin. There is elaborate chiming music on the hour.

Quilting is an old Kentucky craft tradition. Here the Seigel family of Owenton displays many of Rebecca Seigel's award-winning creations.

Ashland Oil Company in Ashland, Kentucky, has one of the largest refineries in the country.

A balloon at sunset drifts near the John A. Roebbling bridge over the Ohio River in Northern Kentucky.

KENTUCKY'S BLUEGRASS

The Bluegrass region lies pretty much in the center of Kentucky, and Lexington lies in the center of the Bluegrass. Roads run out from Lexington like spokes of a wheel to the towns on the rim of the Bluegrass: Paris, Georgetown, Versailles, Harrodsburg, Danville, Nicholasville, Winchester, and just beyond to Frankfort, Lawrenceburg and Mount Sterling.

This was the first region of Kentucky settled, the site of the settlers' fierce battles with the Indians, the state's first constitution, its first college. Here Daniel Boone's Wilderness Road ran up from Cumberland Gap to near Danville. Here Simon Kenton's Limestone Road ran down from the site of his limestone spring near Maysville to become Lexington's Limestone Street.

This is, in a sense, the heart of Kentucky. It is the way Kentucky likes to think of itself. Here live the Clays and Breckinridges, Man o'War and Citation. It is the home of Keeneland, Clay's Ferry, Centre and Transylvania, the University of Ken-

tucky, Claiborne Farm, Shakertown, and the Palisades of the Kentucky River. History and legend lie gently on the Bluegrass, like haze across the graceful acres of its horse farms.

In their early days, these were rough towns, where proud farm owners raced their horses down main streets, gambled, brawled in saloons and, their shallow pride easily offended, stalked with their seconds to street or grove and sounded off against each other with pistols. Near Georgetown, Elijah Craig, a Baptist minister, distilled what some say was the first Bourbon whiskey, and in Lexington, editor John Bradford printed the state's first newspaper, the Kentucky Gazette. The whiskey outlasted the paper.

Wherever you turn in the Bluegrass, history waits close at hand. The homes of Henry and Cassius Clay lie a minute from interstate highways. Jet planes come in low over the station where the Bryants held off Indians. There is a small park in Harrodsburg where James Harrod built a cabin and started the first permanent settlement west of the mountains. In the center of Danville, George Rogers Clark persuaded Kentuckians to opt for statehood.

Go north on Lexington's Broadway a couple of blocks and you will find Transylvania University straddling the street, the stately old Morrison Hall dominating the lawn on your right. This was the first college west of the Alleghenies, the Light in the Wilderness. Here, in the first years of the 19th century, the distinguished educator Horace Holley came to build a great university on the frontier. And he did, and developed a pleasant society with it; too pleasant, perhaps, for he was eventually driven out of town and his college disbanded when hard-eyed Christians complained that he neglected the religious teaching of his students, while spending too much time on balls and races.

Go west on Old Frankfort Pike and you will pass the grand acres of Woodburn Farm, where Robert Alexander brought to Kentucky the first Thoroughbred horses, the first purebred cattle and began a lineage that survives in the Bluegrass today. Until World War II, time seemed to flow seamlessly here, yesterday blending into today without a ripple. There was a time of anguish during the Civil War days, when families of the Bluegrass were often torn apart, as was the state, between North and South, and the dashing Confederate cavalryman John Hunt Morgan came home to rest between his daring, if futile, raids, and the patient Shakers of Pleasant Hill bowed in pain as Union and Confederate troops by turn commandeered the produce of their fields and their labor.

From its earliest days, Lexington has had something of a rivalry with the state's largest city, Louisville. If that rivalry was ever social in nature, it has faded with time. However, a degree of economic rivalry remains. Lexington can point to its more rapid recent growth, its metro government and the desirable cleanliness of its industry as signs of its superiority. But the rivalry today seems to revolve chiefly around UK versus U of L basketball teams. Indeed, it seems to survive more due to the prodding of the media than as a matter of general interest.

Lexington, though, seems to have had the quality of being able to absorb change with ease. With the turning of time, Transylvania, or an offspring, became Centre College, and Kentucky A&M became UK. With a new century, farms grew larger, as did the towns which served them. Hemp replaced corn as a cash crop, and in turn gave way to tobacco. The old turnpikes, most of them privately owned roads whose owners collected tolls that farmers and travellers resented, gave way to the first public hard-surfaced roads, and railroads tied towns and states and regions together. Still, drivers travel over Old Frankfort Pike, and a painful battle has for years divided neighbors over whether to widen, and change forever, the lovely and historic Paris Pike.

But in the end, time and change are one, and with the advent of World War II, change worked its way into the Bluegrass. Industry moved in, first being the impressive blue and white sprawl of IBM, then Square D, then a dozen plants that, in a turning of history, once more saw the advantages of Lexington at the site of the crossroads. The town, and those around it, saw unprecedented growth. In the demand for housing, Paris became an almost bedroom community. Subdivisions pressed against farmland and horse farms. Malls slowly drained the life from Lexington's Main Street, as in the surrounding towns by-passes with their shopping centers sucked traditional trade from the main streets and courthouse squares. UK, expanding to meet the needs of returning veterans, swelled from 5,000 to 20,000 students, and the old Alumni Gym gave way to the Coliseum and then to the cavernous Rupp Arena, and the old Stoll field was razed as football shifted to Commonwealth Stadium.

Change did not stop with the post-war boom. IBM faltered, cutting its employment and lessening its impact on the community, but Toyota came with its huge Georgetown plant, changing not only the region but the state, and assuring that there would be no return to the pastoral past for the Bluegrass. Industry was invading the smaller towns of the Bluegrass, too. Danville organized to

My Old Kentucky Home was made memorable by Stephen Foster's song which is now sung by Kentuckians at major events. The house has been restored to complete authenticity. It is a little known fact that a duel between two Latin scholars was fought on the lower grounds of the house because of a disagreement about the conjugation of a Latin verb.

A spindly legged foal looks for his mom amid the lush pastureland of Fayette County bluegrass. The colt grows quickly into his legs, which are as long at this age as they will ever be.

make sure that it would welcome only non-polluting and stable plants. Lawrenceburg, Harrodsburg and Winchester felt similar growth. Paris and Nicholasville are threatened to become suburbs as Lexington grows outward, and Woodford County residents have organized to save their scenic land from the industry that was starting to spread outward from the town limits of Versailles. In a similar effort to keep growth under control, voters merged Lexington and Fayette County into the state's first metro government.

Fifty postwar years have seen a century of change. Old grads coming back to reunions can hardly find their old school amidst the sprawl and clashing architecture of the UK campus. Its tone and flavor changed with growth, and there are few who can recall the days when tall, dignified President Frank LeRond McVey defended his school with an eloquent warning to the state legislature that you cannot have a great state without a great

university, nor when his wife, Frances Jewell McVey, served tea and finger sandwiches to students on Wednesday afternoons.

Lexington was always a magnet for the people from the Eastern Kentucky mountains, and now coal corporations which have rich holdings in the hills have their headquarters in the town. Calumet and Spendthrift farms, show-places, cornerstones of the thoroughbred industry and of horse legend have changed hands. Coldstream belongs to the University.

The state has moved in with parks at Boonesborough and Harrodsburg to protect the sites of Kentucky's birth. On the outskirts of Lexington the handsome Kentucky Horse Park preserves traditions of the industry and attracts hordes of tourists and locals to its three day events and steeplechases. Ashland, the home of Henry Clay, is open to the public, as is Whitehall, Cassius Clay's old home, now a state historic shrine. The restored Shakertown,

Horse racing is a way of life in the Bluegrass.

Formed as a racing club, the Keeneland Race Course outside Lexington remains a beautiful and unusually genteel track. It still has a clubhouse for members only.

at Mercer County's Pleasant Hill, draws Kentuckians as well as out-of-staters to its disciplined buildings and tree-lined streets where the food, clothing and furniture of the devout, celibate Shakers shows how they lived and worshipped and pursued the quiet tenor of their ways. A small paddle-wheel steamboat on the nearby Kentucky River takes visitors up past the imposing Palisades.

Downstream, Frankfort, the state's capitol, straddles the river, carved into its limestone cup of a valley, distinguished chiefly by the looming Capitol and the graceful Governor's Mansion nearby. Visitors are often surprised to find that the otherwise unimposing small town, rather than the larger Louisville or Lexington, is the state capitol. Kentuckians have often commented on that, too. The unexceptional fact is that the town fathers of Frankfort simply caught the larger cities sleeping and outbid them for the right. But through the years, Frankfort has become an interesting town, with blocks of historic old homes and attractive grounds around the capitol. Except when there is the occasional flood, the town is something of a

tourist spot, with its floral clock, Boone's grave and a marker on the walk outside the Old Capitol where a governor was shot. School children stream in by the busload to traipse through the marble halls and gawk at the legislators, who descend upon the town for 60 days every two years.

It would be nice, for some at least, to be able to say that the more things change in the Bluegrass, the more they stay the same. But that is not true. Broad interstate highways, by-passes and ring roads have replaced meandering pikes. Old Union Station, which once dominated Lexington's Main Street, is gone. One-way Vine Street now runs along the trackbed where the L&N once hissed and smoked its way, bringing back students from vacation and businessmen from the East. There is no L&N today, no Southern. But Bluegrass Field, between Lexington and Versailles, ties the region to the world, as once did the steel rails.

It is still said that you can tell people from Eastern Kentucky who make fortunes because they all live in Lexington. This is not strictly true. But the interstates and Mountain Parkway have linked the eastern towns closer to Lexington. The flavor of the mountains still mingles with the scent of newly mown bluegrass. And the hub of the Bluegrass wheel, now only minutes from its rim, is still a major reason why people love to live in the heart of Kentucky.

One of the last bastions of southern formality, Keeneland still requires proper attire.

Every year, serious "reenactors" perform a realistic enactment of the battle of Perryville, the largest one fought in Kentucky during the Civil War. General Bragg led Confederate forces against General Buell's Union army. The battle was considered a draw but Bragg withdrew his troops from the state.

Shelley Richardson, the mistress of Elmwood Inn, operates a bed and breakfast with her husband, Bruce. The Inn is located at the site of the battle of Perryville and served as a hospital for both sides after the battle.

Around 1820, the first thoroughbreds and trotters were brought to Woodford County, Kentucky, by R.A. Alexander whose great-great granddaughter, Kathy Brewer, still lives at Woodburn, the family horse farm. During the Civil War, Quantrill's Raiders, including Frank James, stole a number of trotters from the farm but overlooked the famous thoroughbred, Lexington, from whom many race horses are descended.

Woodburn. The original tract of land has been in the family for seven generations.

The Lincoln Memorial in Hodgenville celebrates the birthplace of the sixteenth president. It is visited by thousands each year, including a host of international visitors. Lincoln only lived here a few years, but Kentucky claims him as a native son and intends to keep him.

The Vietnam Memorial in Frankfort is an unusual design. As the earth rotates, the shadow of the sun dial falls on the birthday of each Kentuckian who fell in that war.

What appears to be an abandoned fort is really an abandoned distillery. The Old Taylor facility in Franklin County has just recently emptied its warehouses after many years of producing Bourbon whiskey.

The Abbey of Gethsemane is home to the largest and oldest order of Cistercian monks in the country. The Trappist Monastery was home to the writer, theologian and philosopher Thomas Merton, and is also known for its cheeses and Bourbon-laced fruitcakes. Here, a monk walks through the cemetery.

A common sight in Kentucky: a man and his horse.

Shakertown is a restored village near Harrodsburg in central Kentucky where the members of the Shaker religious sect maintained a settlement from the 1820s to the early 1900s. Given the name "Shakers" because of the trembling that attended their devotional dancing, they believed in simplicity, pacifism, celibacy and separation from the world. The community is located on 2,700 acres of beautiful rolling land above the Kentucky River.

Daniel Boone is buried on a site in Frankfort overlooking the Kentucky River and the Capitol. When Boone died, he was living in Missouri and there was some controversy between the two states about where his final resting place should be located. Some Missourians say that he was never taken back to Kentucky, but most Kentuckians don't believe it.

Midway, Kentucky is just that, located between Lexington and Frankfort. A railroad track runs through the center of the well preserved old town which can take care of all of your antique needs. During the Civil War, guerrillas and renegades from both sides stole horses from neighboring farms.

Wild Again at Three Chimneys farm in Woodford County is a very successful stallion in a business requiring perpetuation of the pedigree.

Ashland was the home of Henry Clay, the Great Compromiser, who served as the Speaker of the House of Representatives, a United States Senator and the Secretary of State. Schoolchildren from Lexington pose on the steps of the mansion where Clay lived from 1811 until his death in 1852.

*Gentlemen of Bardstown
take lunch at the Talbott
Tavern, which has
poured Bourbon
produced from the
surrounding distilleries
since 1792.*

The courthouse at Paris in Bourbon County was the center of activity in the past. The county was not named for the whiskey, though it was first distilled not far away, but for the Bourbon families of France.

Shelbyville, Kentucky.

The state capitol in Frankfort, modeled after the post-Civil War nation's capitol in Washington, D.C.

Near Richmond, Kentucky, is Whitehall, the home of Cassius Clay, the famous abolitionist, Ambassador to Russia, and duelist. When Clay was in his eighties he married a 15 year old girl, inspiring a local posse to find out if she were a captive bride. Clay met them at the door fully armed and from the second story window the bride allowed she would not leave Whitehall. Later, when he refused to pay taxes, another posse went out to arrest him and was met with a hail of gunfire. The sheriff reported that he thought they could take the house if the governor would send some cannon and troops to make an attack upon the virile old man.

Whitehall, the home of Cassius Clay in Richmond, stood empty for 65 years after his death in 1903. A grandson purchased a great part of the original tract from various Clay descendants and the Commonwealth of Kentucky bought the land in 1968 and fully restored it. Guided tours are provided on a daily basis.

University of Kentucky basketball fans are very serious about their team and do not tolerate losing seasons. Here, a fan demonstrates her feelings about a play gone wrong.

The enormous Rupp Arena in Lexington

Transylvania Seminary was chartered in 1780 by the Virginia Assembly on 8,000 acres taken from British Loyalists. First classes were held in Danville, Kentucky, but the school was soon moved to Lexington where it ultimately became Transylvania University. Graduates include Jefferson Davis, Confederate General Albert Sidney Johnston, President of Texas Stephen Austin, two U.S. Vice Presidents, 36 governors of various states, and 50 U.S. Senators.

The courthouse at Newcastle, sometimes written New Castle, is typical of the imposing courthouses throughout the state. There are 120 counties in Kentucky and each has a courthouse within a day's horseback ride of the residents of the county. The automobile may have ended the need for this convenience but no county has voted to merge with another.

The statue of Governor William Goebel stands in front of the old Capitol in Frankfort near the spot where he was assassinated in 1900. Hundreds of mountaineers were brought down from Eastern Kentucky to protect the interests of the Republicans, but the Democrat Goebel became the victim. Secretary of State Caleb Powers and Big Jim Howard were tried, convicted, jailed, and released after the Court of Appeals overturned their convictions. Later, Powers served as a Congressman for eight years.

A craftsman at Fort Harrod, Harrodsburg, Kentucky.

This cabin near Hodgenville is a replica of the boyhood home of Abraham Lincoln.

A replica of a part of the 1774 Fort Harrod, which was the first English settlement west of the Allegheny Mountains. Now known as Harrodsburg, the area includes a cabin believed to have been where Abraham Lincoln's parents were married.

EASTERN KENTUCKY

The mountains of Eastern Kentucky may be the most scenic part of a scenic state, a region of steep, rocky hills and brooding hollows, laced with a hundred streams, a land of parks and lakes, national forests and waterfalls. This is the country to which the Long Hunters, Finley, Boone and Gist, came before the land had a name. They were followed by settlers who pushed on to the central plateau that became the Bluegrass, leaving the hills secluded and silent until, in the 1790s, the settlers started turning right after they passed through Cumberland Gap, trudging up the valleys of the Kentucky and Cumberland Rivers, while others were turning from the Ohio River down the Big Sandy River into the mountains.

So less was written and less was known about the narrow valleys of the eastern mountains than about the Bluegrass or the settlements along the Ohio. That suited the mountain people just fine. They wanted no part of the seaboard cities. They had fled the oppressive rule of English kings and the fast-growing cities along the Atlantic, seeking a new freedom in a new land, seeking in the remote hollows the right of a man, standing on his own land, to make his own rules.

The region variously referred to as Eastern Kentucky, the mountains, Appalachia, is a rough land. The nature of its terrain is implied by the narrow passes which cut through its hard ridgelines, Cumberland Gap, Pound Gap, Hagan Gap; by its looming rocks, the Pinnacle, Raven Rock, Pilot Rock, and Lonesome Pine. The names of its places and streams reflect impressions of a people in a new and often harsh land, Frozen Creek, War Branch; Bullskin, Quicksand, Troublesome, but also a land that touched the warmth, Beauty, Lovely, Pippa Passes.

The remoteness of the moutains, not so much in distance as in time needed to travel, east to Washington or Richmond, west to Lexington or

Cincinnati, for years shut out the world for many mountain dwellers and, equally hurtful, gave the growing American beyond the mountains a partial, often distorted, picture of the mountaineer. There were, undeniably, people in the secluded hollows who deserved the caricatures in the northeastern press of the ignorant, illiterate, one-gallus hick, in slouch hat and tattered overalls, his jug of moonshine liquor on his hip, his trusted rifle at the ready. But there were also entrepreneurs who built towns, roads, and mills, made great fortunes from rich salt wells, founded schools in the wilderness and sent their sons back east to college, doctors and lawyers, men who became powerful in state government and in Congress.

Yet, fairly or not, the hills from the Ohio River to Tennessee, from Virginia to the Bluegrass, became identified with violence. Why the beautiful hills became the battlefield for the bloody feuds that ripped the region in the years before and after the Civil War is a question historians and sociologists have pondered for a century. But it happened. They tore families and neighborhoods, towns and counties apart. They defied the efforts of lawmen to control them, often drawing the lawmen into the fighting. They led to the murder of Governor William Goebel, the only American governor ever assassinated in office, and launched Kentucky into the 20th century on a wave of bitterness and hatred, creating for the state an image of violence that stained and hampered it for decades.

It was Big Jim Howard, a reluctant player in the great Clay County War, who was convicted for the killing of Goebel, though many still doubt his guilt. But the rage of mountain Republicans over what they charged was the theft of the election by Goebel Democrats, and Democratic anger over the killing of their governor blasted a rift between the mountains and the rest of the state that has been slow to heal. It robbed the mountain citizens of influence and power in state government and cost them, in turn, state help in building roads, bridges, schools and public structures.

It is rough land, and man has dealt roughly with it, ripping away the thin earth of its hills with hillside farms, with roughshod logging and mining that left the soil bare to the rains that sluiced down the hillsides, flooding the rivers and sending them smashing through the towns of the valleys.

It is a land of great wealth, and men have grown wealthy here, though much of the wealth was taken by outsiders who left scarred land for those remaining, who found the living hard. John C.C. Mayo built the greatest fortune and the finest mansion in the hills from coal lands that he bought for pennies and sold for dollars. The grisly French-Eversole feud erupted, in part at least, because Joe Eversole objected to the buying practices of Fulton French who, representing eastern land companies, bought the mineral rights to the land of unsuspecting mountain dwellers for pennies per acre.

Whether in the logging camps of the earlier days or the more recent coal mines, work and life in the hills have often been hard. Yet the people of Eastern Kentucky have seldom willingly left the hills. When the loggers left and the sawmills closed, when the coal mines went through their cycles of boom and bust, the people went north by the thousands and tens of thousands to find work. But when times improved and word filtered north of jobs opening in the towns along the mountain valleys, back they came, turning their eyes once more toward the hills of home.

This has always been a hard land in which to build highways and railroads. Its surface is as crumpled as wadded paper. You can trudge forty miles through hollows to reach a town five miles away as the crow flies. In the early days many towns depended on flooding rivers to carry their produce downriver to market, because moutain roads cost mountains of money. If roadbeds are built high enough above the valley floor to keep out floods, they often must be cut through the sheer rock of the hillsides. And the sparse populations of mountain towns have made it hard to justify roads to link them. Under the hills of Harlan County once lay the greatest coal deposits east of the Mississippi, but there was no hard surfaced road into Harlan until 1928. Before 1960 there was not a mile of four-lane highway in all of Eastern Kentucky.

Yet men have come here dreaming great dreams. On the slope of the cemetery overlooking Middlesboro stands a large gray stone, facing out over the valley toward the Pinnacle of Cumberland Gap, and it bears the name Arthur. It is the resting place of that doughty Scot, Alexander Arthur, cousin of President Chester A. Arthur and founder of the city of Middlesboro. He, too, dreamed great dreams. In the late spring of 1886, Arthur came through the Gap looking for minerals, and in the hills beyond the Gap found what he believed to be huge deposits of coal and iron. He immediately envisioned in the beautiful valley another Midlands, a Pittsburgh of the South. Hurrying to England, he formed the American Association, Ltd., bought up thousands of acres of land along the Kentucky - Tennessee border and began to build the city that would be the heart of his empire. He called it Middlesborough.

Middlesborough did not grow, it sprang full-blown from the head of Alexander Arthur. By its second year, when the L&N Railroad pushed south from Pineville, it had a population of 17,000.

Streets were laid out in a grid, with such English names as Dorchester and Salisbury. A broad-streeted business district took shape, as did a fine residential area for executives. Soon the town boasted the second golf course in America, while on the hill overlooking the town stood the Middlesboro Hotel, at the time among the finest hostelries in the country. When it opened, a special train brought in champagne, quail, oysters, and hummingbird tongue. Ward MacAllister, the social arbiter of New York, led the grand march. Jenny Lind, the famed Swedish Nightingale, sang, while in the valley below, miners, railroad men and construction workers drank and fought in a spirited imitation of the Old West.

But Arthur had made a mistake; he built his town of wood, and one night the entire place burned to the ground. Hastening back to England, he raised some more money and rebuilt in brick. But fate was waiting. The sudden failure of the Baring Bank of London practically bankrupted Arthur, and as the money ran out, so did the iron ore he had overestimated. Within weeks a hush came over the town. The mines closed, grass grew along the rail lines. The furnaces shut down. Still hoping, Arthur raced to New

The original Kentucky Fried Chicken restaurant, founded by Harland Sanders, is still operating in Corbin, Kentucky. Initially, Sanders started out with a motel and gas station on Route 25 to catch the traffic heading to and from Florida.

York to find new investors. He couldn't, and as the years passed, the dream slowly died. In 1912, so did he. In his will he asked to be buried in Middlesborough (now Middlesboro,) and there, on a gentle hillside overlooking the city of his faded dreams, he rests.

On the south end of the town, at the foot of Cumberland Gap, a giant tunnel is being bored to carry the highway through, rather than over, the mountain trail that Boone and his settlers followed. The National Park Service is planning to return the mountain pass to the pristine condition Boone found when he looked to the opening land to the West.

For here in the mountains, surviving depression, recession, floods and the boom and bust of coal, there remains the beauty of the hills, the healing, comforting sight of mountains, and here remains, too, the stubborn determination of the people of Eastern Kentucky not to be driven from their land. When it became obvious that the people of Pikeville would either move their town or see it destroyed by the flooding Big Sandy River, a visionary mayor, William Hambley, decided to move the river instead. And that they did, cutting the whole, towering mountain above the town in two, and routing the river, along with the highway and railroad, through the massive cut, filling in the old riverbed to serve as land for homes and business.

A four-lane highway now tops the floodwall which protects Pineville from the Cumberland River floods that threatened to wipe the town off the map. The town is rebuilding , and is still the site, each May, of the lovely Mountain Laurel Festival that salutes the beauty queens of each of Kentucky's colleges, and the blooming of the white-pink mountain wildflower. Towns along Interstate 64 and 75 are growing in population and in employment in the new factories.

A tough land bred a tough people.

An historical marker outside Sanders Cafe notes the birthplace of Kentucky Fried Chicken.

Shooting matches and basketball goals are two important traditions in Powell County.

Clogging is a traditional mountain dance; young and old participate.

Tom and Pat Gish and their families publish the Mountain Eagle, *a crusading weekly in Whitesburg, Kentucky that has taken on strip miners, politicians, and powerful school superintendents. Their strong editorial opposition to strip mining in the early 1970s resulted in the newspaper being burned down by hired thugs. The arsonists were ultimately caught by a county sheriff when he overheard them bragging about their deed. Several were tried and convicted, but only received probation. The* Mountain Eagle *has won many journalism awards and is studied frequently in college journalism courses.*

The Natural Bridge at Red River Gorge is 900 tons of ancient rock suspended across a span of mountain side. At one time there were proposals by the Corps of Engineers to flood part of the Gorge, which is a 25,662-acre stretch of beautiful country in the Daniel Boone National Forest near Slade, Kentucky. There was such an outcry of protest, lead by Supreme Court Justice William Douglas, among others, that the concept died a quiet death.

The fall colors in Eastern Kentucky draw state park visitors from all over the country.

Fundamental religion is evidenced by this sign in Floyd County.

(Above) Cloggers at Natural Bridge State Park. (Below) The ol' swimming hole at Lake Cumberland State Park.

Fishermen work Rowan County's Cave Run Lake, where the muskie run.

Joe Begley, who is part Indian, runs a general store in the tiny crossroads of Blackey, in Letcher County, where you can find a little bit of everything. He is a passionate mountaineer strongly opposed to the volatile issue of srip mining and was often allied with Tom Gish of the Mountain Eagle and the late writer, Harry Caudill, in conservation battles. The last time Joe left Letcher County was to attend a signing of the Federal Strip Mining bill in the White House during Jimmy Carter's presidency.

At the courthouse in Harlan, Kentucky, an honor roll of coal miners killed in the mines since 1912 stands like a war memorial. It is said that a man's life wasn't worth as much as a mule in the early mining days, as men would be sent to places where the life of a mule would not be risked.

Along the tracks at the city depot in Evarts, Kentucky, in 1931, 300 striking miners ambushed 10 deputies and a non-union replacement worker. Four men were killed in the ensuing fight, adding to the bad blood and lore surrounding mine/miner conflicts.

William McCool has worked in the mines of Perry County, near Hazard, for over 20 years. The deep mine seam he works is over four miles in a horizontal direction.

Coal, the economic staple of much of Eastern Kentucky.

This small coal town in Letcher County just west of Whitesburg is typical of the area. The coal industry has been greatly depressed for a number of years and, as always, the small towns lose their young people who seek employment elsewhere.

In 1877, the Nadda Tunnel in Campton, Kentucky, near the Red River Gorge in Powell County was cut by hand using only picks and shovels.

Paschal Fields has been running his gas station in Whitesburg for many years and still uses an old-fashioned system of book-keeping.

Mountain children in Stanton, Kentucky, warily greet visitors.

Pineville boys take a midday break, chewing some tobacco and logging a little conversation.

Harlan County was known as "bloody Harlan" in the '30s and '40s when the United Mine Workers and the company men engaged in many a shoot-out. The National Guard was sent into the area on several occasions to maintain the peace. The hardware store across the street from the courthouse proclaims that "undertaking" is available in addition to the standard consumer goods.

Arthur Asher is 93 years old and has lived in Cave Run Valley since 1916. In the 1930s, he and other Pineville boys hauled the "chain" (see back cover) to the top of the Pineville Mountain and created the legend that it had to be chained, else it would fall on the town of Pineville. They were operating as the unofficial Pineville Tourist Office.

Barton Hensley, Sr. founded the Hensley Settlement in Bell County around the turn of the century. It featured a self-sufficient agricultural life style on top of the mountain. Here is the schoolroom for the settlement, whose population reached a high of 100 people in 1925. Following World War II, the community dwindled to just a few farmers.

Outside Pineville, Kentucky, a farmer and mule continue to till the land the old-fashioned way.

Change comes slowly but surely to the mountains.

Morehead State University.

Handmade quilts are a popular item in Berea, the craft capitol of Kentucky.

The mountains at dusk.

The legendary Adolph Rupp once said that when he needed basketball players, he would "raise his eyes and look unto the mountains" for help. These boys practice in Letcher County.

Cumberland Falls is just a short distance from Corbin, Kentucky. Except for Niagara Falls, this is the largest waterfall east of the Rockies.

WESTERN KENTUCKY

It would be easier to describe Western Kentucky if someone could decide where it is. Even the people who live there can't agree on where it begins, though it obviously ends with the Mississippi. And no one seems to know where the expression "West, by God, Kentucky" came from. Ask someone who lives west of Bowling Green where he is from and, likely as not, he will say, "West, by God, Kentucky." That may indicate regional pride, pugnacious pride, defensive pride, or none of the above.

Some say that Western Kentucky begins with the Mammoth Cave region, which is not a bad place to begin. Any region should be proud to claim it, for the cave itself is one of those natural world wonders, and millions of people troop through its caverns and the surrounding national park each year. There are more than 300 miles of caves in the area, and Mammoth cave is only one of them. Others, such as Onyx, are smaller than Mammoth, but some are more colorful, though some geologists speculate that all of the caves in the region around Cave City and Horse Cave are parts of one vast system of caves that honeycomb the limestone underlying the region west of Glasgow and north of Bowling Green.

This is divided country. A man in Elkton or Hopkinsville may claim that Western Kentucky begins with what used to be the Land between the Rivers (the Cumberland and Tennessee Rivers) and is now the Land Between the Lakes (Barkley and Kentucky lakes.) Others say they live in the Pennyroyal (or Pennyrile), an imprecise region that takes up a lot of Western Kentucky, but begins as far east as the eastern coalfields. Incidentally, the Pennyrile is named for a small blue flower that grows in the region like a weed, but people purporting to know say there are two types, the other a kind of mint that can be used in juleps and has made Elkton the mint julep capital of the country (presumably this does not include Louisville at Derby time).

Western Kentucky can be divided into any number of parts. There is the Jackson Purchase, which stretches from the lakes to the Mississippi. There can't be much arguing about its boundaries. It was purchased by Andrew Jackson from the Indians and is bounded by rivers and Tennessee. It contains Columbus - Belmont State Park, where, during the Civil War, Confederate forces tried to bar Federal gunboats from the Mississippi by stretching a huge chain across the river. The chain sank. The gunboats sailed on by. Back to the old drawing board. But the park is beautiful, a little gem. Fancy Farm, also in the Purchase, lies west of Mayfield and would probably be ignored except for the Fancy Farm Picnic, to which hopeful politicians trek on the first Saturday in August to eat, shake hands, sweat and speak to the throngs that troop to the Picnic chiefly to hear them.

Then there are the coalfields, which center around Muhlenburg County and continue up through Madisonville to the north. A plaintive song bemoans the fact that a native son cannot go back to Muhlenberg County, since trains carrying out strip-mined coal have hauled it away. Actually, there is some left, though as the song implies, it is hard to find traces of a village named Paradise.

People from around Bowling Green go up to Louisville on business or to performances at the Center for the Arts, and people from the whole region go to Lexington to see ball games, though they have their own teams at Western Kentucky University and at Murray State University. But a lot of trade goes outside. The Franklin-Bowling Green-Russellville-Hopkinsville region "drains", as they say, down to Nashville, Tennessee; whereas shoppers from the Purchase often go to Memphis, and those from around Paducah sometimes travel up to St. Louis. Henderson does a lot of cross-river trading with Evansville, Indiana, but Owensboro, the biggest town in Western Kentucky (if it is actually in Western Kentucky) does a lot of trading with Louisville. So does Madisonville.

Just as Eastern Kentucky was hotly pro-Union in the North - South "disagreement" known as the Civil War, so was Western Kentucky a stronghold of the Confederacy. In fact, Russellville was at one time the Confederate capitol of the state, in defiance of Frankfort. It also has the only bank that advertises the fact that it was once robbed; it even has a mural depicting the robbery by the Jesse James Gang in 1868 (there is some dispute over whether Jesse was actually involved) and each year there is a big to-do with a re-enactment of the robbery.

The Bibb family lived in Russellville, and Major Bibb developed Bibb lettuce which, like beauty, is its own excuse for being. Marine Lieutenant Presley O'Bannon, who planted the flag on the shores of Tripoli during the war with the Barbary pirates and gave the Marine Corps the basis for its hymn, was born in Russellville. For some reason he is buried in Eminence, in Henry County.

Hopkinsville is widely known as "Hoptown," but the city fathers don't care much for the nickname. It was a center of the Black Patch War, when, in 1904, tobacco farmers rebelled against the tobacco trust, led by James Duke, and burned barns and warehouses in an effort to hold tobacco off the market until the companies would pay them a decent price. The leader of the farmers was tried but, being a home-town boy, was acquitted.

Western Kentucky is big farming country. Down around Todd, Logan and Christian counties they raise a lot of tobacco, and corn is a big crop up through Union and Livingston. At one time there was a lot of cotton raised in the counties along the Mississippi, and as far north as Mayfield, which is still heavily agricultural. Paducah, home of famed author and humorist Irvin S. Cobb and named for the Indian chief Paduke (who, most historians concede, never existed) is the largest town in the Purchase, although Murray, with its university and growing industry, is beginning to challenge it.

Some Western Kentuckians dismiss Owensboro, Henderson, Smithland and Paducah as river towns, and they are, but they are in Western Kentucky, too. Owensboro is an industrial town, not to mention a college town, while neighboring Henderson is smaller and quieter. It was, for a time, the home of the famed nature artist John James Audubon, and Audubon State Park, named in his honor, is located in Henderson and houses many of his original paintings.

Rivers, the Cumberland, Tennessee, Green and Tradewater, not to mention the bordering Ohio, lace Western Kentucky and have always been important in its development. Today the Tennessee and Cumberland are impounded to form Barkley and Kentucky lakes and the Land Between the Lakes. This area is administered by the Tennessee Valley Authority and is one of the biggest recreational areas in the world, drawing millions of visitors each year. Four state parks, Kentucky Dam Village, Barkley, Kenlake and Chickasaw, make the region a magnet for tourists and sportsmen, and the area around the western shore of Kentucky Lake is becoming a favored spot for retirement homes. There are two other lake-based state parks, Pennyrile and Lake Malone, farther east.

Smithland, county seat of Livingston County, is a curious little town, sitting right on the bank of the Ohio. It sits so close that at one time half of the main street just fell off into the river. Indeed, you might say that Smithland clung to the river too long. In the 19th century it was a busy river port, flourishing from the trade of steamboats plying the Ohio and nearby Cumberland Rivers. When the new-fangled railroads started pushing their rails across the land, the people of Smithland sniffed that rails would never replace steamboats and refused to grant the railroad a right-of-way through their town. Paducah made a better guess of things to come, granted the right-of-way and got the railroad. Paducah grew. Smithland withered. Today it has about 400 people. Paducah is a small city.

There is a strong note of tragedy in the history of Livingston County. Here, in the early 1800s, came Lucy Lewis, a sister of Thomas Jefferson, and

Lake Barkley Lodge is a popular tourist spot.

her sons, Isham and Lilburne. The Lewis brothers were moody, haughty men, trying to re-establish the Virginia plantation way of life along the Ohio, and were also given to hard drinking. Enraged when a slave boy broke a pitcher, they tied the boy to a kitchen table, took an axe and, calling their slaves together to witness, hacked the pleading, screaming boy to pieces, throwing the remains into the fire. They hid the skull in a section of the chimney they built to conceal the grisly pieces, but that night, as though nature was recoiling in horror, the great New Madrid earthquake shook the region, causing the Mississippi to flow uphill, forming Reelfoot Lake and, incidentally, knocking down the chimney and dislodging the skull of the murdered slave boy. The skull was found, the facts were uncovered, and the brothers were indicted for murder. Rather than endure prison, they met by night at their hillside graveyard and agreed to kill themselves. Lilburne did, but Isham lost his nerve, ran off into the night and was captured and

In Fairview, Kentucky, just west of Elkton, there is a 351 foot obelisk marking the birthplace of Jefferson Davis, the only president of the Confederacy. It stands in dramatic contrast to the rolling countryside and is only two feet shorter than the Washington Monument in the District of Columbia. This Western Kentucky area was strongly sympathetic to the Confederacy and sent many horses and men to the cause.

Hospitable and gracious Joy Boone, poet, critic, and writer, and her husband, George, a historian and lawyer, live in Elkton, Kentucky, in a home that has been in his family since 1813. The Boones host an annual literary study of Robert Penn Warren, novelist and national poet laureate, who was born about 12 miles away in Guthrie.

jailed. He escaped and was later reported to have gone to Louisiana, where he was killed in the Battle of New Orleans. The foundations of the mansion built by Jefferson's nephews can still be seen on top of a hill near Smithland, overlooking the Ohio.

The western part of the region makes up the First Congressional District of Kentucky, which has long been known as the Gibraltar of Democracy, and has sent to Washington such Democratic stalwarts as Senator Alben Barkley, who became Franklin D. Roosevelt's Vice President, , and Congressman Noble Gregory. The counties to the east are part of the Second District, which was strongly Democratic for 125 years, and was represented in Congress by the redoubtable William Natcher of Bowling Green for 40 of those years until his death in 1994. None of this answers the question of why people say they are from West, by God, Kentucky.

Canoeing on the Green River, which winds its way through the cave area of Kentucky.

Kentucky Lake is 150,000 acres of impounded water in Western Kentucky, making it one of the largest man-made lakes in the world. Because the lake is not surrounded by high hills, the sailing is excellent.

Owensboro, Kentucky, is the headquarters of the International Bluegrass Music Association. During the year it hosts many musical events, such as those shown on these pages.

Kentucky country hams are unsurpassed in taste, despite the claims of upstart neighboring states and their "sugar-cured" hams.

High school football is a big Friday night activity, like here in Fulton, Kentucky.

Western Kentucky is the breadbasket of Kentucky, with farmers growing corn, wheat, soybeans, and until recently, cotton.

The bird hunting is fine in Western Kentucky, even for ducks and geese, which have repopulated to a great degree on the Mississippi flyway.

The Banana Festival in Fulton, Kentucky.

Murray State University.

Amish children near their community in Crittenden County.

They fire up the coals on a regular basis in Owensboro, the Barbecue Capitol of Kentucky. Unlike many places, mutton is often the favorite choice of meat here.

In 1868, the James Gang, either with or without Jesse, robbed the Southern Deposit Bank in Russellville, Kentucky, of $17,000. The president of the bank had once assisted Robert James, the father of Jesse and Frank, to become a Baptist minister. Several days after the robbery, $9,000 was mysteriously deposited into the bank. The mural in the existing bank depicts the robbery and is probably the only bank in the country to show such an event on its walls.

(Left) Markers to the graves of two Cherokee Indian chiefs who died on the infamous Trail of Tears were discovered in Hopkinsville in 1954. Steve Shields, a local sculptor, created two poignant statues of the chiefs, Whitefly and Fly Smith. The Trail of Tears began in 1838 in North Carolina, Georgia, and Tennessee when 16,000 Cherokees were summarily rounded up by the U.S. Army and marched to reservations in the Oklahoma territory. Over 4,000 died on the march.

Bowling Green, Kentucky, is the home of General Motors' sporty Corvette plant. Recently, the one millionth Corvette rolled off the production line. A Corvette Museum will open soon.

This might look like Mark Twain, but he's really a professor at Kentucky Wesleyan University in Owensboro.

Virginia Petty, the Whistling Woodcarver, makes a variety of spoons, ladles, scoops and utensils from wood near her home near Smith's Grove.

World-famous Mammoth Cave has more than 330 miles of explored passageways, making it the longest known cave system in the world.

In the mountains, we rested in the shade of walnut,
then walked all day toward the rolling grasslands.
Nowhere had we seen a land more cunning—
with green, green fields and sky of cornflower.
In two hundred years should the engine's roar
awaken the buffalo who led us here,
we should be glad to awaken also
to walk with you your rolling pastures
and see again the evening sky
ablaze with peach and redbird.

Maureen Morehead